The Visual Guide to

Asperger's Syndrome and Emotions

by Alis Rowe

Also by Alis Rowe

One Lonely Mind
978-0-9562693-0-0

The Girl with the Curly Hair - Asperger's and Me
978-0-9562693-2-4

The 1st Comic Book
978-0-9562693-1-7

The 2nd Comic Book
978-0-9562693-4-8

The 3rd Comic Book
978-0-9562693-3-1

The 4th Comic Book
978-15086839-7-1

The 5th Comic Book
978-15309879-3-1

Websites:
www.alisrowe.co.uk
www.thegirlwiththecurlyhair.co.uk
www.womensweightlifting.co.uk

Social Media:
www.facebook.com/thegirlwiththecurlyhair
www.twitter.com/curlyhairedalis

The Visual Guide to

Asperger's Syndrome and Emotions

by Alis Rowe

Lonely Mind Books
London

For people on the autism spectrum
and their loved ones

hello

Emotions can be tricky for everyone. We all need to know how to manage our emotions, but how exactly this is done is often implied rather than taught.

One of the main issues I face is that my emotions tend to be atypical. I don't always feel the same way others do about the same situations. This makes it hard to know how to react to people and for them to know how to react to me. Other people just have to be patient. To talk to understanding and non-judgmental people helps, but otherwise I tend to remain quiet and detached.

Another thing is that the emotions I feel are very strong. But I don't think that trying to stop the emotion helps me, I think the key is to manage my behaviour when I have that emotion, and remind myself that the emotion will pass and get less as time goes by.

I hope this book helps you to recognise, label, understand and manage your own emotions.

Alis aka The Girl with the Curly Hair

Contents

RECOGNISING EMOTIONS

Defining empathy

Empathy is, at its simplest,
being able to share the feelings
of another

THERE IS A PERSISTENT STEREOTYPE THAT PEOPLE ON THE AUTISTIC SPECTRUM CANNOT FEEL EMOTIONS AND LACK EMPATHY

THE GIRL WITH THE CURLY HAIR DOESN'T BELIEVE THIS IS THE CASE

SHE THINKS THIS STEREOTYPE HAS COME ABOUT BECAUSE OF THE DIFFICULTY IN RECOGNISING, UNDERSTANDING AND COMMUNICATING EMOTIONS, RATHER THAN AN INABILITY TO FEEL THEM

Something very important to understand is that A PERSON WITH ASD may not know - or be able to tell someone - how they are feeling at any given moment

Many of us just assume that everybody can just very easily recognise and express emotions

HERE ARE SOME OF THE REASONS WHY EMOTIONS CAN BE VERY DIFFICULT FOR PEOPLE WITH ASD

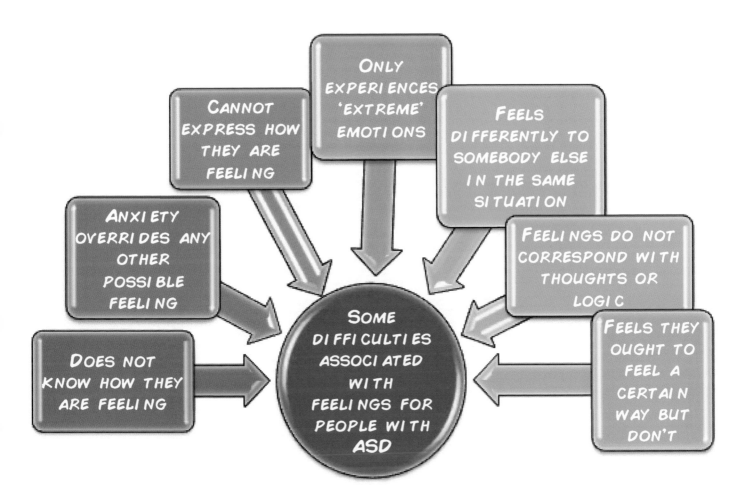

ONLY EXPERIENCES 'EXTREME' EMOTIONS

CANNOT EXPRESS HOW THEY ARE FEELING

FEELS DIFFERENTLY TO SOMEBODY ELSE IN THE SAME SITUATION

ANXIETY OVERRIDES ANY OTHER POSSIBLE FEELING

FEELINGS DO NOT CORRESPOND WITH THOUGHTS OR LOGIC

DOES NOT KNOW HOW THEY ARE FEELING

SOME DIFFICULTIES ASSOCIATED WITH FEELINGS FOR PEOPLE WITH ASD

FEELS THEY OUGHT TO FEEL A CERTAIN WAY BUT DON'T

Social etiquette says that we're supposed to say "fine" every time somebody asks us how we are, so it's easy to see why emotions can be confusing!

The Girl with the Curly Hair has developed quite a sophisticated awareness of her own emotions. This book aims to help people with ASD to understand their emotions too

19

In this book, we will think about:

Is the person on the spectrum aware of their emotions?

What does an emotion look/feel like?

Can they label the emotion with the right word?

How is this emotion processed?

It is very hard for me to explain my difficulties to others. I do not always have the right language to explain, or it might take me a while, or I might manage to express my difficulties but show no emotion about them

People tend to forget that actually explaining or expressing something is very, very hard in itself

Common emotional responses in ASD

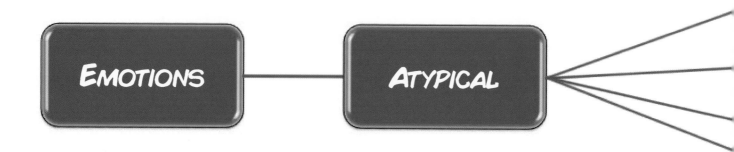

DOESN'T FEEL THE SAME WAY AS A NEUROTYPICAL PERSON ABOUT THE SAME SITUATION

FEELS THE SAME WAY AS A NEUROTYPICAL PERSON ABOUT THE SAME SITUATION, BUT THE EMOTION THEY ARE EXPERIENCING IS MUCH MORE INTENSE OR LESS INTENSE

FEELS THE SAME WAY BUT EXPRESSES IT IN A CONFUSING OR UNEXPECTED WAY

IS SLOW TO FEEL OR EXPRESS AN EMOTION

An important thing to understand is that PEOPLE ON THE AUTISTIC SPECTRUM tend to have very intense emotions (many describe them as being "all or nothing"; or if the scale of the emotion was measured between 0 and 100, 100 would be reached immediately)

A NEUROTYPICAL PERSON may find it helpful to imagine how it might be to experience very strong emotions the way that PEOPLE ON THE AUTISTIC SPECTRUM do. If your emotions were very strong, you would likely be driven to show corresponding very strong behaviours, e.g.

Feeling	Examples of strong behaviours
Anger	Hitting, shouting, fighting, aggression...
Anxiety	Running away from things, avoiding things, a strong desire to be alone, difficulty leaving the house, compulsions
Happy	Laughing, difficulty settling, being very loud, flapping...
Disappointment	Crying or suddenly bursting into tears

PEOPLE WITH ASD MIGHT ALSO HAVE EITHER DIFFERENT EMOTIONS ABOUT A SITUATION FROM THE 'EXPECTED NEUROTYPICAL RESPONSE', OR VERY STRONG EMOTIONS ABOUT SOMETHING THAT DOESN'T REALLY PROVOKE A RESPONSE IN A NEUROTYPICAL AT ALL

PERHAPS MANY OF THE 'CHALLENGING' BEHAVIOURS DISPLAYED BY PEOPLE WITH ASD HAPPEN BECAUSE THE PERSON IS EXPERIENCING A VERY STRONG EMOTION. PERHAPS IF THEIR EMOTIONS WERE NOT AS OVERWHELMING, IT WOULD BE EASIER FOR THEM TO CONTROL THEIR BEHAVIOURS

ALSO, IF THE PERSON IS EXPERIENCING AN ATYPICAL EMOTION, THEIR BEHAVIOUR IS PROBABLY GOING TO BE ATYPICAL TOO, HENCE IT'S EASY TO LABEL THE PERSON AS BEING CHALLENGING

I HAVE A DELAYED EMOTIONAL REACTION TO THINGS. PEOPLE MIGHT SOMETIMES THINK I DON'T CARE, OR THAT I'M UNEMOTIONAL. BUT REALLY IT JUST TAKES ME A BIT LONGER TO PROCESS AND UNDERSTAND A SITUATION BEFORE I CAN REACT TO IT PROPERLY
I OFTEN FEEL ISOLATED WHEN AROUND/WITH OTHERS BECAUSE OF OUR DIFFERENT REACTIONS TO THINGS, E.G. I'M USUALLY NOT OFFENDED OR UPSET BY THINGS THAT OFFEND OR UPSET OTHERS, NOT EXCITED BY THINGS THAT EXCITE OTHERS... ETC.

Lack of empathy?

It's more like: experiencing the same situation in a different way, therefore struggling to have the same feelings as SOMEONE ELSE

AND

Anxiety is one of the most common responses to absolutely anything! It's hard to feel other things when the overwhelming emotion is anxiety

HERE ARE SOME EXAMPLES OF THINGS THAT TEND TO MAKE OTHER PEOPLE EXCITED OR HAPPY, BUT THAT MAKE THE GIRL WITH THE CURLY HAIR FEEL VERY ANXIOUS...

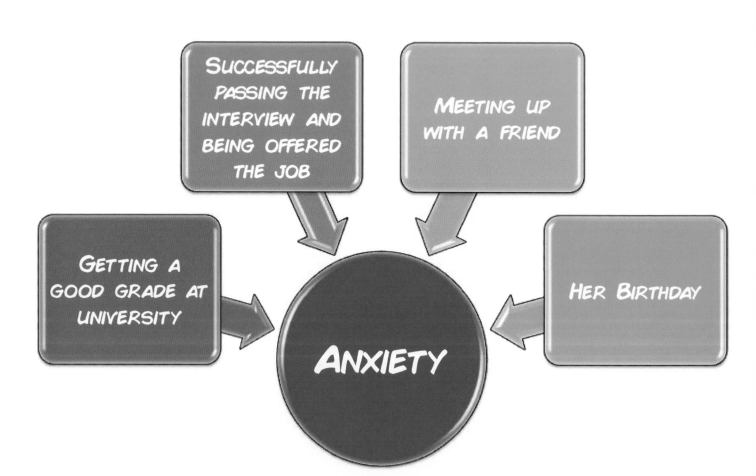

THE GIRL WITH THE CURLY HAIR
THEREFORE FINDS IT HARD TO EMPATHISE
WITH SOMEONE'S EXCITEMENT ABOUT A
SITUATION THAT SHE FEELS ANXIOUS ABOUT

Why is anxiety such a common response?

The Girl with the Curly Hair often just feels 'neutral'

Most of the time, when she is alone and following her routine, there's no overwhelming emotion, just a state of feeling settled and neutral and getting on with things

As soon as something 'happens' – even if it's a good thing – this changes that neutral feeling and instead causes instability, which leads to anxiety

ANXIOUS

- THE SITUATION HAS NOW CHANGED
- NO LONGER SETTLED
- THERE IS A TRANSITION IN MOOD STATE FROM NEUTRAL TO ANXIOUS (TRANSITIONS ARE HARD AND CREATE THEIR OWN ANXIETY!)
- NEW THINGS TO PROCESS AND THINK ABOUT

- WORKING
- STUDYING
- READING
- LIFTING WEIGHTS
- EATING
- BEING IN THE MOMENT...

NEUTRAL

SOMETHING HAPPENS THAT CHANGES 'THE MOMENT'

It can take some time before anxiety changes to excitement/ happiness

It takes The Girl with the Curly Hair a while to process and come to terms with things

Only once she has thought about the *IMPACT* of the circumstance can she begin to feel excited/ happy about it

 **EVENT HAPPENS** **ANXIETY** **EXCITEMENT /HAPPINESS**

IMMEDIATE/ SHORT TERM REACTION

LOTS OF TIME SPENT THINKING ABOUT THE IMPACT, E.G. "HOW IS IT GOING TO AFFECT ME? WHAT EXACTLY IS GOING TO CHANGE? WHAT IS GOING TO HAPPEN BEFORE AND AFTER THE EVENT HAS OCCURRED?"

SO IF I DON'T GET THIS TIME, AND IF MY QUESTIONS AREN'T ANSWERED, I WILL STRUGGLE TO EVER FEEL EXCITED OR HAPPY ABOUT WHATEVER THE 'EVENT' IS

HERE ARE A FEW EXAMPLES OF ANXIETY RESPONSES FROM *THE GIRL WITH THE CURLY HAIR* WHERE THE OTHER PERSON EXPECTED HER TO FEEL 'EXCITED'

HER NEUROTYPICAL PARTNER BOOKS TICKETS FOR THEM...

SHE TELLS A FAMILY FRIEND ABOUT
HER FANTASTIC UNIVERSITY RESULTS...

37

SHE FINDS OUT SHE GOT THE JOB
THAT SHE HAD APPLIED FOR...

CAN YOU SEE HOW THESE SITUATIONS COULD HAVE BEEN MADE LESS ANXIETY-PROVOKING FOR HER?

HER ANXIETIES NEED TO BE ADDRESSED *BEFORE* SHE CAN FEEL EXCITED...

IDENTIFYING, SCALING AND COMMUNICATING EMOTIONS

Use your body!

Learn to understand the signs and symptoms you experience when you are feeling a certain way

This will be very individual. Here are some examples:

Emotion	Signs (things other people might observe)	Symptoms (things that the person with ASD may experience)
Happy	Smiling, being very chatty	Feeling "weightless," "glowing", "warm"
Anxious	Going very quiet, talking too much, pacing around, flapping hands, rocking, head banging	Butterflies in stomach, headache, difficulty breathing, increased rate, wanting to go to the toilet, feeling sick
Sad	Crying, tearful	Tight chest and throat, eyes prickling and watery
Anger	Shouting, hitting, kicking, red face, frowning	"Going to 'explode'", "a volcano erupting inside", tight jaw, clenching fists

You could create a book of notes or drawings of things that have historically evoked all the different emotions (it will help the person with ASD to better understand their own feelings and can help to develop their emotional vocabulary to help others better understand them)

This can be a good tool for working on developing an understanding of the greater spectrum of emotions, e.g.

ANXIOUS

All corn flakes gone
Speaking on the phone
Group work

CROSS

When teacher/personal
trainer/therapist is late

IT'S ALSO AN INTERESTING TOOL BECAUSE IT CAN OPEN UP DISCUSSIONS AS TO HOW DIFFERENT PEOPLE MIGHT FEEL ABOUT THE SAME SITUATION, E.G.

A NEUROTYPICAL PERSON COMES DOWNSTAIRS TO EAT CORN FLAKES AT BREAKFAST AND THERE ARE NO CORN FLAKES LEFT. HE FEELS... DISAPPOINTED

THE GIRL WITH THE CURLY HAIR FEELS... ANXIOUS

SOME PEOPLE LIKE TO USE PICTURES OF FACES TO HELP THEM UNDERSTAND AND COMMUNICATE EMOTIONS

I AM

Sometimes it's hard to link how you are feeling with a particular situation. Working with a list can help...

Step 1. Choose a situation

Lesson | Homework | (Friends) | Teacher | Something Else

Step 2. Narrow it down even more

Jane | Daisy (Both of them) Something Else

Step 3. What are the physical/verbal signs?

Smiling | Crying | Being very chatty | (Going very quiet)

Step 4. Link the signs or symptoms to the feeling

anxious

These steps will help a person learn how to recognise and label emotions

As discussed at the beginning of this book, PEOPLE WITH ASD often feel very intense emotions

Or they might be feeling a less strong emotion but can only *COMMUNICATE* the strong one

And working out exactly what situation evoked which feeling can be really hard too

It can be useful to help PEOPLE understand that there are various degrees of emotion and that not ALL situations will cause an *INTENSE* emotional response

THE SIMPLEST TOOLS SUCH AS A BASIC NUMBER SCALE...

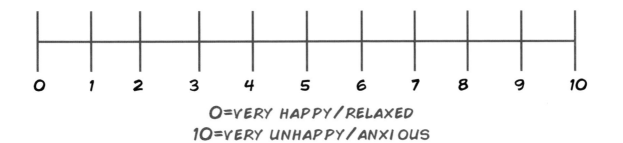

0=VERY HAPPY/RELAXED
10=VERY UNHAPPY/ANXIOUS

OR A THERMOMETER SCALE...

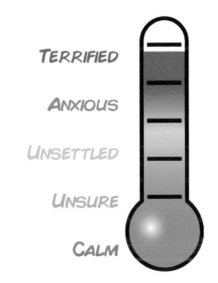

TERRIFIED

ANXIOUS

UNSETTLED

UNSURE

CALM

CAN BE VERY HELPFUL IN TEACHING SOMEONE TO KNOW INTENSITY OF A FEELING AT ANY GIVEN MOMENT

The Girl with the Curly Hair really likes The Volcano Concept:

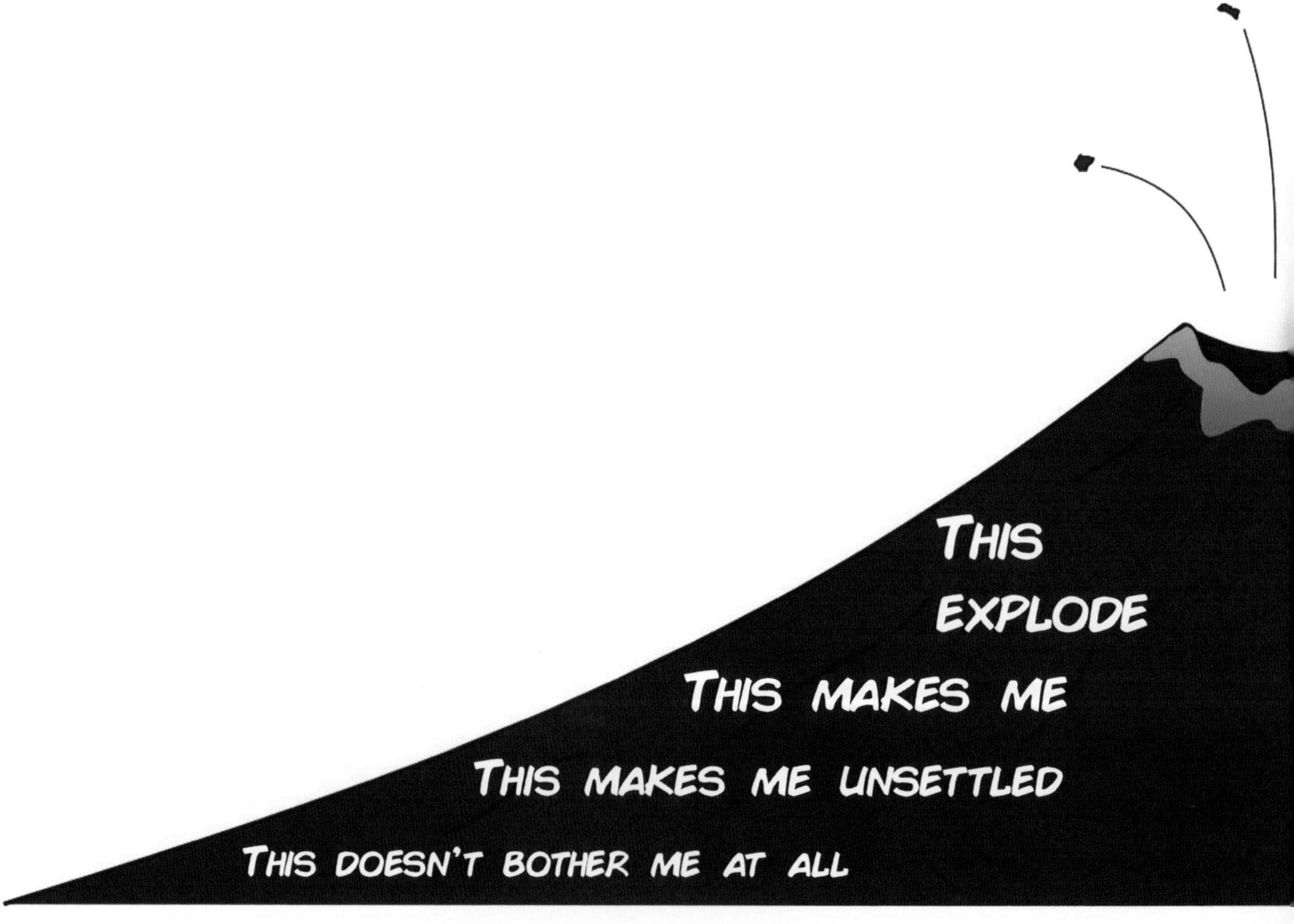

MAKES ME

VERY ANXIOUS

57

Tools such as The Volcano Concept allow her to really *PINPOINT* which aspects of a situation are unbearable for her and think about the ways these could be improved

It also shows her that no situation is completely **ALL** bad

There might be some difficult parts, but there may be good parts too

Situation – Appointment with social worker	This doesn't bother me at all	This makes me unsettled	This makes me very anxious	This makes me explode
Arrival			X	
Questions they ask me		X		
The appointment taking too long			X	
Eye contact		X		

BUT I REALLY LIKE THAT I'M NOW GETTING THE SUPPORT I NEED

If a person has a particular interest, you could even think about how you could incorporate that into how they recognise and label emotions. For example, a person who likes dinosaurs...

Emotion	Label
Happy	Pterosaur
Anxious	Stegosaurus
Sad	Diplodocus
Anger	Tyrannosaurus Rex

LOVED ONES CAN CHECK IN THEIR LOVED ONES WITH ASD REGULARLY

Recognising when it's time to stop and rest

People with ASD may have a tendency to push themselves too much because they struggle to recognise signs of stress, illness or depression, etc.

This can lead to burnout

Teaching yourself or the person with ASD what common signs are of, for example, stress overload, can be extremely helpful

Stress overload

Cognitive
- Memory problems
- Inability to concentrate
- Poor judgment
- Seeing only the negative
- Anxious or racing thoughts
- Constant worrying

Emotional
- Depression or general unhappiness
- Anxiety and agitation
- Moodiness, irritability, or anger
- Feeling overwhelmed
- Loneliness and isolation
- Other mental or emotional health problems

Behavioural
- Eating more or less
- Sleeping too much or too little
- Withdrawing from others
- Procrastinating or neglecting responsibilities
- Using alcohol, cigarettes, or drugs to relax
- Nervous habits (e.g. nail biting, pacing)

Physical
- Aches and pains
- Diarrhea or constipation
- Nausea, dizziness
- Chest pain, rapid heart rate
- Loss of sex drive
- Frequent colds or flu

Stress Symptoms, Signs and Causes. (n.d.).
Retrieved from: https://www.helpguide.org/articles/stress/stress-symptoms-signs-and-causes.htm

NOTE HOWEVER, THAT SOME OF THESE THINGS MAY BE 'NORMAL' FOR ASD ANYWAY, E.G. "ANXIETY" AND "LONELINESS" ARE COMMON IN ASD BUT DON'T NECESSARILY MEAN A PERSON IS "CLINICALLY DEPRESSED" FOR EXAMPLE

LOOK AT THE WHOLE PICTURE AND ALL THE SYMPTOMS. LEARN WHAT IS 'NORMAL' AND 'HEALTHY' FOR YOU AND OBSERVE WHEN YOUR NORMAL CHANGES

Determining when you are too sick, too tired or simply not well enough to engage in activities can be tricky for those on the spectrum. It is very difficult to understand when "too" tired is too tired, or "too" sick is too sick

THE OTHER PROBLEM IS... PEOPLE MAY BE TIED TO THEIR ROUTINES EVEN WHEN THEIR ROUTINES ARE NOT THE BEST THING FOR THEM AT THAT TIME

The following flow chart was designed to help PEOPLE ON THE AUTISTIC SPECTRUM to make a decision when you find it hard to make a decision of your own accord

It might help you to first work out your own signs and symptoms for the three major feelings: 1) stressed/anxious 2) unsure 3) excited. Everyone has different signs, but it's important to try to identify yours and what they mean for you

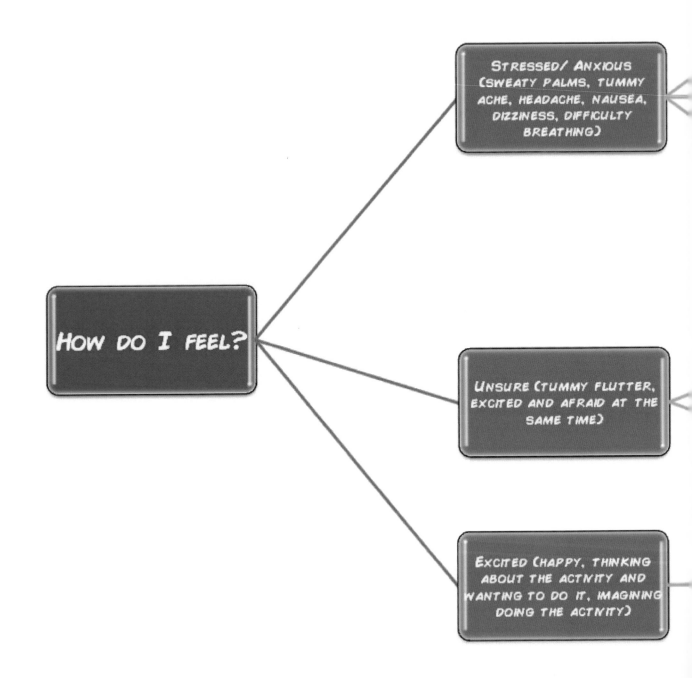

(BIG THANKS TO NELE MUYLAERT FOR THE FLOW CHART)

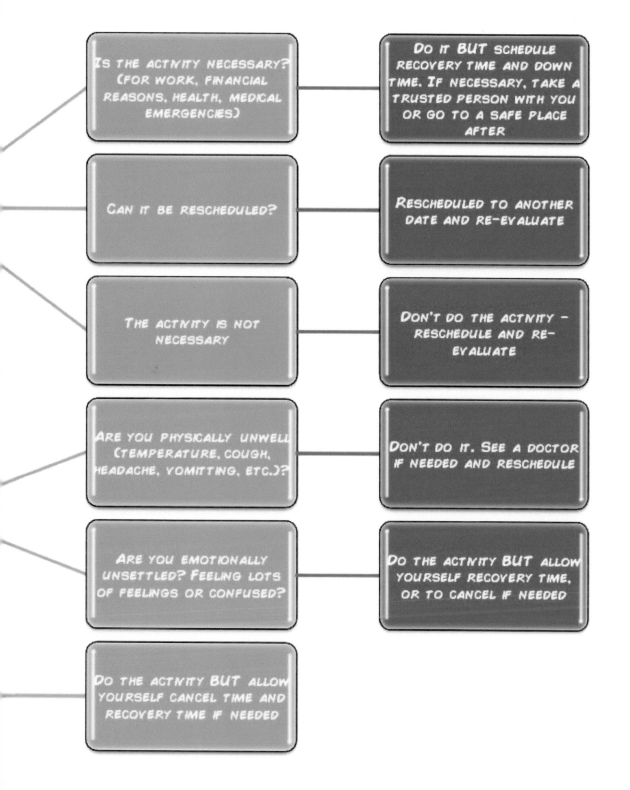

IS THE ACTIVITY NECESSARY? (FOR WORK, FINANCIAL REASONS, HEALTH, MEDICAL EMERGENCIES)

DO IT BUT SCHEDULE RECOVERY TIME AND DOWN TIME. IF NECESSARY, TAKE A TRUSTED PERSON WITH YOU OR GO TO A SAFE PLACE AFTER

CAN IT BE RESCHEDULED?

RESCHEDULED TO ANOTHER DATE AND RE-EVALUATE

THE ACTIVITY IS NOT NECESSARY

DON'T DO THE ACTIVITY - RESCHEDULE AND RE-EVALUATE

ARE YOU PHYSICALLY UNWELL (TEMPERATURE, COUGH, HEADACHE, VOMITTING, ETC.)?

DON'T DO IT. SEE A DOCTOR IF NEEDED AND RESCHEDULE

ARE YOU EMOTIONALLY UNSETTLED? FEELING LOTS OF FEELINGS OR CONFUSED?

DO THE ACTIVITY BUT ALLOW YOURSELF RECOVERY TIME, OR TO CANCEL IF NEEDED

DO THE ACTIVITY BUT ALLOW YOURSELF CANCEL TIME AND RECOVERY TIME IF NEEDED

73

PROCESSING EMOTIONS

THE GIRL WITH THE CURLY HAIR THINKS THERE IS ONE PARTICULAR METHOD OF EMOTIONAL PROCESSING THAT IS IMPORTANT TO UNDERSTAND

Anxiety and overwhelm!

Sometimes just the feeling of anxiety or overwhelm is so strong that it overrides any other emotion and prevents a PERSON from properly engaging in the situation they are in

Anxiety can be really debilitating - it can prevent people from thinking and communicating properly and it's very exhausting

This anxiety is the default emotion

It's very quick and intuitive

But what it means is that participating in situations is very, very hard

The consequence is that a person can't enjoy things, can't concentrate or perform optimally, and might say things they don't really mean

SOMETIMES I DON'T THINK VERY MUCH AT ALL DURING SOCIAL SITUATIONS, I JUST FEEL ANXIOUS AND OVERWHELMED. ONLY LATER DO I THINK ABOUT WHAT HAPPENED, WHAT THE OTHER PERSON SAID, WHAT I COULD OR SHOULD HAVE SAID, ETC.
I THINK VERY MUCH ABOUT HOW I AM FEELING. IF I AM OVERWHELMED OR ANXIOUS, I JUST THINK "I FEEL ANXIOUS AND OVERWHELMED. I NEED TO GET OUT OF HERE"

ANXIETY OR BEING OVERWHELMED MEANS A PERSON MAY NOT REALLY SAY OR BEHAVE IN THE WAY THEY WOULD HAVE HAD THEIR ANXIETY BEEN LESS

THE GIRL WITH THE CURLY HAIR HAS LEARNED STRATEGIES THAT CAN HELP...

INSTEAD OF IMMEDIATELY RESPONDING TO PEOPLE, SHE OFTEN SAYS THINGS LIKE...

I'M NOT SURE, I'LL HAVE TO THINK ABOUT THAT

CAN I GET BACK TO YOU ABOUT THAT?

I'LL TEXT YOU LATER

OTHER PEOPLE CAN HELP BY BEING PATIENT AND INVITING THE PERSON WITH ASD TO TAKE THEIR TIME WHEN THINKING AND RESPONDING TO THINGS, SUCH AS...

HAVE A THINK AND LET ME KNOW

NO NEED TO REPLY IMMEDIATELY

WOULD LOVE TO KNOW WHAT YOU THINK ABOUT --- WHEN YOU HAVE TIME

Managing Emotions by Managing Thoughts

OUR FEELINGS, THOUGHTS AND BEHAVIOURS ARE ALL LINKED:

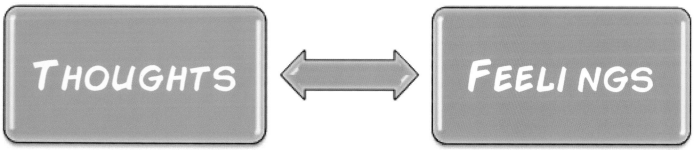

FOR EXAMPLE, WHAT HAPPENS WHEN THE GIRL WITH THE CURLY HAIR WAKES UP AND THINKS:

IT'S GOING TO BE ANOTHER HORRID DAY

THOUGHTS
- NEGATIVE
- GLOOMY
- SELF-CRITICAL

FEELINGS
- SAD
- DEPRESSED
- TIRED

BEHAVIOUR
- WITHDRAW
- ISOLATE

A VICIOUS CYCLE ENSUES, LEADING TO THE MAINTENANCE OF LOW MOOD AND ANXIETY

SO, SHE HAS THIS THOUGHT "IT'S GOING TO BE ANOTHER HORRID DAY", WHICH MAKES HER FEEL SAD AND HOPELESS. THIS THEREFORE MAKES HER STAY IN BED, NOT EVEN BOTHERING TO DO THE THINGS SHE NORMALLY ENJOYS (NOT EVEN WEIGHTLIFTING!)

ALL OF THIS JUST MAKES HER FEEL *WORSE*

SHE CAN VERY EASILY *CHALLENGE* THIS THOUGHT HOWEVER:

CAN YOU SEE THAT THIS THEN MAKES HER FEEL BETTER AND MEANS SHE'S MORE LIKELY TO DO THE THINGS SHE LIKES?

WHAT HAPPENS WHEN THE GIRL WITH THE CURLY HAIR THINKS:

This makes her feel sad and lonely. When she goes out, she doesn't talk to anyone, she avoids eye contact and she has a grumpy expression on her face

All of this just makes her feel worse and puts people off approaching her who would have otherwise smiled and said hello!

She can very easily *CHALLENGE* this thought:

LET ME THINK OF ALL THE PEOPLE WHO LIKE ME... THERE'S MUM, DAD, SISTER, THE BOY WITH THE SPIKY HAIR, DAISY, THE LADY WHO WALKS THE DOG, MY LOVELY NEXT DOOR NEIGHBOUR...

MY WEIGHTLIFTING COACH THINKS I AM FANTASTIC

I HAVEN'T SEEN DAISY FOR A WHILE, I WILL TEXT HER

I COULD TRY TALKING TO SOME OF THE PEOPLE AT THE GYM

Thinking in a more balanced way about the reality of the situation and finding a more helpful thought is a good strategy

The Girl with the Curly Hair is collecting helpful thoughts that she can then evaluate and decide which one works best for her

MANAGING EMOTIONS BY MANAGING BEHAVIOUR

THERE MAY BE DIFFERENT RELATIONSHIPS BETWEEN THOUGHTS, FEELINGS AND BEHAVIOUR...

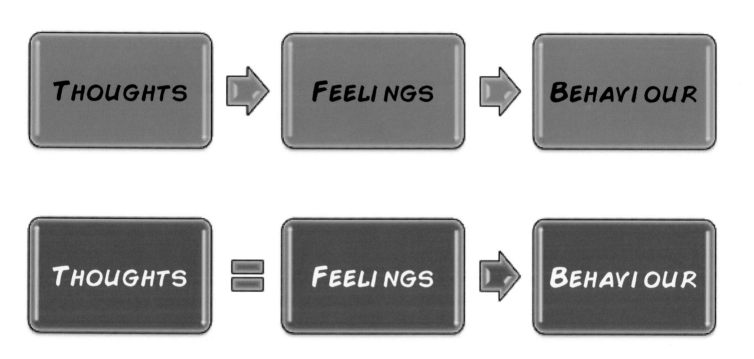

PERHAPS NEUROTYPICALS ARE MORE PRONE TO THE GREEN PROCESS, AND PEOPLE WITH ASD THE BLUE ONE

FOR EXAMPLE, THE GIRL WITH THE CURLY HAIR IS IN HER OFFICE. LOTS OF PEOPLE ARE AROUND AND SHE FEELS VERY ANXIOUS. SHE THINKS:

I FEEL VERY ANXIOUS

IN THIS INSTANCE, THE FEELING IS SO STRONG THAT ALL SHE CAN THINK ABOUT IS THE FEELING

WHEN SOMEONE IN THE OFFICE EATS A B.A.N.A.N.A., SHE THINKS:

THAT'S REVOLTING, I FEEL SICK

AGAIN, THE FEELING IS SO STRONG, IT TAKES UP ALL HER THINKING

It's much more difficult to change a feeling than it is to change a thought

Thoughts can be illogical and untrue

Feelings are never illogical or untrue. Feelings are always very real

Another strategy is to therefore manage your feelings

THE GIRL WITH THE CURLY HAIR THINKS THAT THERE IS ONLY ONE WAY TO SUCCESSFULLY MANAGE FEELINGS... AND THAT IS TO **ALLOW** HERSELF TO HAVE THEM AND TO **BE KIND TO HERSELF**

IT IS ALSO HELPFUL FOR HER TO REMEMBER THAT FEELINGS DO PASS. FEELINGS ARE NOT PERMANENT

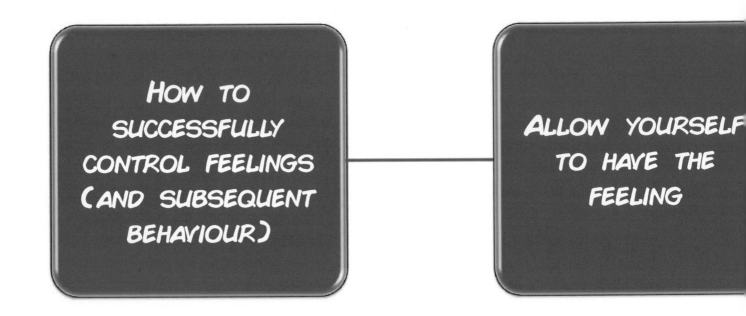

How to successfully control feelings (and subsequent behaviour)

Allow yourself to have the feeling

DO NOTHING IN PARTICULAR (DISCONNECT ACTIONS FROM FEELINGS)

DO SOMETHING CONSTRUCTIVE/ HELPFUL

DOING NOTHING IN PARTICULAR BUT JUST ALLOWING YOURSELF TO HAVE THE FEELING CAN HELP

OFTEN MY EMOTIONS ARE SO STRONG THAT ALL I CAN DO IS DISCONNECT FROM THEM. HENCE I DISPLAY A CALM, DETACHED PERSONA. IF I EXPRESSED SUCH STRONG EMOTIONS, MY BEHAVIOURS WOULD NOT BE APPROPRIATE...

IT'S OK TO BE ANXIOUS, IT'LL PASS

Not allowing yourself or another person to have the feeling can lead to destructive/unhelpful behaviours. This can include 'bottling things up' which never works out well

It also creates a lack of trust in the relationship which can lead to weak communication, struggling to get close or relate to anyone, leading to loneliness and masking

EXAMPLES OF *NOT ALLOWING ANOTHER PERSON TO HAVE A FEELING*

Examples of allowing another person to have a feeling

HERE IS AN EXAMPLE OF
SOME HELPFUL VS UNHELPFUL
(CONSTRUCTIVE VS DESTRUCTIVE)
WAYS IN WHICH THE GIRL WITH THE
CURLY HAIR COULD EXPRESS ANGER

Anger

Constructive / helpful

- Lift heavy weights / go for a run / exercise
- Describe your thoughts and feelings to someone who will be empathetic and listen
- Rip paper up
- Throw ice cubes in the bath
- Write a song or poem

Destructive / unhelpful

- Hurting yourself
- Hurting someone else
- Alcohol / smoking / over or under eating
- Bottling things up

OFTEN, KNOWING *HOW TO BEHAVE* WHEN YOU HAVE A FEELING IS NOT INTUITIVE – YOU COULD CREATE A BOOK OR A TABLE OR A CHART, E.G.

WHEN I FEEL...	...WHAT CAN I DO THAT IS HELPFUL?
HAPPY	CONCENTRATE LEARN WORK HAVE FUN BE INVOLVED WITH PEOPLE
ANXIOUS	STROKE MY CAT TAKE A BREAK TAKE DEEP BREATHS SQUEEZE MY SHOULDERS
SAD	DO SOMETHING I ENJOY STROKE MY CAT TELL SOMEONE
ANGER	MOVE AWAY FROM PEOPLE TAKE DEEP BREATHS RIP UP PAPER HIT A PILLOW THROW ICE CUBES IN THE BATH

THE GIRL WITH THE CURLY HAIR HAS 4 MAIN STRATEGIES TO HELP REDUCE THE INTENSITY OR LIKELIHOOD OF A NEGATIVE FEELING:

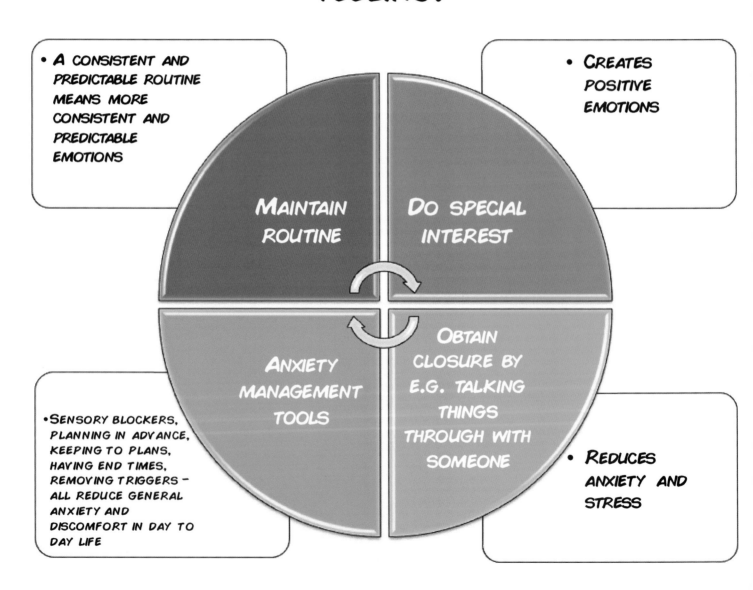

- A CONSISTENT AND PREDICTABLE ROUTINE MEANS MORE CONSISTENT AND PREDICTABLE EMOTIONS

- CREATES POSITIVE EMOTIONS

- SENSORY BLOCKERS, PLANNING IN ADVANCE, KEEPING TO PLANS, HAVING END TIMES, REMOVING TRIGGERS – ALL REDUCE GENERAL ANXIETY AND DISCOMFORT IN DAY TO DAY LIFE

- REDUCES ANXIETY AND STRESS

MAINTAIN ROUTINE

DO SPECIAL INTEREST

ANXIETY MANAGEMENT TOOLS

OBTAIN CLOSURE BY E.G. TALKING THINGS THROUGH WITH SOMEONE

Summary of Managing Emotions

Recognise the emotion you are feeling
(e.g. body signs, or refer to your emotion
dictionary book)

Allow yourself to have that feeling (very
important!) and be kind to yourself

Learn how to change your thoughts and change
your behaviour

Take some time out, or behave in a constructive/
helpful manner rather than a destructive/unhelpful
one

Find someone who will validate your feelings

Always remind yourself that feelings are
temporary and that they will pass

Many thanks for reading

Other books in The Visual Guides series at the time of writing:

Asperger's Syndrome
Asperger's Syndrome: Meltdowns and Shutdowns
Asperger's Syndrome in 5-8 Year Olds
Asperger's Syndrome in 8-11 Year Olds
Asperger's Syndrome in 13-16 Year Olds
Asperger's Syndrome in 16-18 Year Olds
Asperger's Syndrome for the Neurotypical Partner
Asperger's Syndrome: Social Energy
Asperger's Syndrome and Anxiety
Asperger's Syndrome: Helping Siblings
Asperger's Syndrome and Puberty
Asperger's Syndrome: Meltdowns and Shutdowns (2)
Adapting Health Therapies for People on the Autism Spectrum

New titles are continually being produced so keep an eye out!